APPETIZERS

APPETIZERS

DELICIOUS FIRST COURSE, STARTER AND ANTIPASTI RECIPES

This edition published in 2010

LOVE FOOD is an imprint of Parragon Books Ltd

Parragon
Queen Street House
4 Queen Street
Bath BA1 1HE, UK

ISBN: 978-1-4454-1365-5

Printed in China

Photography by Günter Beer
Home economy by Stevan Paul
Internal design by Fiona Roberts
Introduction and additional recipes by Christine McFadden

Notes for the reader
• This book uses imperial, metric, and US cup measurements. Follow the same units of
measurement throughout; do not mix imperial and metric. All spoon measurements
are level: teaspoons are assumed to be 5 ml, and tablespoons are assumed to be 15 ml.
Unless otherwise stated, milk is assumed to be full fat, eggs and individual vegetables are
medium, and pepper is freshly ground black pepper.
• The times given are an approximate guide only. Preparation times differ according
to the techniques used by different people and the cooking times may also vary from
those given. Optional ingredients, variations or serving suggestions have not been
included in the calculations.
• Recipes using raw or very lightly cooked eggs should be avoided by infants, the
elderly, pregnant women, convalescents, and anyone with a chronic condition. Pregnant
and breastfeeding women are advised to avoid eating peanuts and peanut products.
• Vegetarians should be aware that some of the ready-made ingredients used in the
recipes in this book may contain animal products. Always check the packaging before use.

CONTENTS

Introduction

Antipasti have been part of Italian culture for centuries—in ancient Rome a meal would begin with a gustatio, *or tasting, of pickled vegetables, olives, and nuts.*

During the middle ages, the aristocracy held massive banquets involving hours of preparation. In order to keep the guests sober enough to appreciate the meal to come, chefs developed the practice of serving a selection of small foods, not only to blot up the drink but also to whet the appetite.

What was eaten depended on geographical region as well as culture. In the fertile plains of the north, dairy products and beef were common; in the hot, arid south, the diet was more frugal, based on olive oil, vegetables, fish, and cheeses made from sheep or goats' milk. Coastal areas obviously made the best use of seafood, while further inland and in mountainous areas cured meats were an important part of the cuisine. Each region had, and still has, its own bread—big-holed, chewy ciabatta in the north, dense unsalted white bread in Tuscany, and gigantic crusty wheels of rough country bread in Puglia in the south. Even today, Italians love to chat over a glass of wine, but to do so without something to nibble is anathema to them.

Regional variations

Although each of Italy's twenty regions remains fiercely proud of their individual culinary identity, similar antipasti dishes are found throughout the country. However, there are variations that occur from town to town, village to village, or even between families—everyone convinced that their particular way of preparing a dish is the best.

Classic antipasti dishes are preserved meats; *salumi* (not to be confused with the cured pork sausage *salame*) and pickled or raw vegetables. Seafood of various sorts is also common. Bread is always served, either as toasted *bruschette* or *crostini* with savory toppings, or on its own for mopping up tasty juices.

Cured meats

In Italy there are literally hundreds of different types of *salame*, each with variations in texture, size, and seasoning. Tuscan *salame* often contains fennel seeds, while further south it comes spiked with chilies. Enthusiasts insist that the best comes from *Felino* in the province of Parma.

Proscuitto crudo is rosy pink, air-cured ham that by law must be dried in the rarefied breezes of Emilia Romagna, Veneto, Piedmont, and Lombardy regions of northern Italy. The best-known are Parma ham and San Daniele. *Coppa*, perhaps less well-known, is made from cured pork neck and has a characteristic marbling of fat running through deep red meat. Pancetta is a type of fatty bacon made from salted belly pork, either smoked or unsmoked.

There are regional *salumi* specialities too, often served individually to showcase the quality: *bresaola* is air-cured beef from Valtellina, *speck* is salted and smoked bacon from the Dolomites, and *culatello* is a very special ham made from pork rump, produced in the Parma area. The gargantuan, pistachio-flecked *mortadella* sausage is a Bolognese speciality, while melt-in-the-mouth *lardo* comes from the mountains above *Cararra* in Tuscany. It is made from pork back fat aged in marble tubs with salt, pepper, and local herbs.

Vegetables

Homes in rural areas of Italy traditionally have a cantina or cellar stocked with jars of preserved vegetables ready to serve as antipasti. Mushrooms, baby artichokes, and tomatoes are usually oil-cured (*sott'olio*), whereas more densely fleshed produce such as carrots, celery, and onions are pickled in vinegar (*sott'aceti*). Grilled, baked, or stuffed vegetables are also served as antipasti.

Pinzimonio is a wonderfully tasty antipasto of raw vegetables cut into strips or chunks and served with a dip of olive oil, sea salt, and cracked black pepper. The vegetables typically include celery, carrots, fennel, radishes, scallions, baby artichokes, and bell peppers—any that are crisp and refreshing.

Bagna càôda (meaning warm bath) is a traditional dip for raw vegetables in Piemonte in north-west Italy. Made with olive oil, anchovies, and a lethal amount of garlic, it is kept warm over a spirit burner in the middle of the table and served with a vast platter of vegetables.

Fish and seafood

Seafood antipasti are extremely popular in Italy's coastal regions. There is a fantastic variety—octopus, mussels, and cuttlefish as well as prawns and crayfish and many more. Italians also like small fish such as sardines, anchovies, and baby mackerel. Seafood is always simply prepared to appreciate the fresh flavors at their best.

Bruschetta and crostini

In their simplest forms, *bruschetta* and *crostini* are no more than thick slices of unsalted bread toasted over a fire and rubbed with olive oil, garlic, and sea salt. Originally from the central regions, these tasty antipasti are now served all over Italy. Toppings vary according to region, but chicken liver pâté and diced tomatoes are among the most popular.

The key to successful antipasti is to limit yourself to a few simple dishes and to buy the best ingredients you can afford. That way, the quality of the food speaks for itself and there is no need for complicated preparation.

Antipasti are essentially improvised and casual—a style of eating that is ideal for busy people who want to eat well but have neither the time nor inclination to cook a traditional hot meal every day. Many dishes can be prepared a day or so in advance and, indeed, will improve with keeping. The flavors of vegetables and pulse-based salads mellow and round out if left to marinate in olive oil, herbs, and a splash of vinegar or lemon juice. Other dishes can be prepared in minutes—a selection of cold meats and pickled vegetables, or Parma ham and melon take no time to arrange attractively on a plate.

Prepared in generous amounts and handed round on big serving platters, antipasti are the perfect food for sharing.

What to serve with antipasti

Though most of the recipes in this book are meals in themselves, you might want to serve some simple smaller dishes as well.

Sauces such as *aïoli, pesto,* or *salsa verde* can be bought ready-prepared and nowadays are of good quality. These make excellent dips or condiments for perking up cold poultry, fish, and mildly flavored vegetables. There are also tasty vegetable purées made from artichokes or aubergines, as well as bottled baby artichokes, onions, and mushrooms, and semi-dried tomatoes and bell peppers. They are all handy to have in the pantry ready for putting together an impromptu platter of antipasti.

Also worth having are salted or vinegar-cured caper buds and caper berries. The tiny green buds have an acidic but mild flavor that make an appetizing garnish scattered over cold meats or fish. The larger, meatier berries are a good appetizer served on their own or mixed with a bowl of olives.

Good crusty bread, preferably from an artisan baker, is essential for mopping up tasty juices, or for dipping in a saucer of fruity olive oil. A selection of breads such as *focaccia, ciabatta, Pugliese,* and tomato bread looks great in a mixed basket. Crispbreads such as *grissini* or the sheet-like *carta di musica* from Sicily are perfect for scooping up dips and sauces.

Always use best quality extra virgin olive oil. Oils from central or southern Italy have a fuller flavor with a peppery finish, whereas those from further north—Liguria or the lakes around Como—are lighter both in flavor and color. It is interesting to serve a saucer of each type so that guests can appreciate the difference as they dunk their bread.

Balsamic vinegar is often used for dipping bread, but it is much better as a delicious sweet-sour seasoning trickled over poultry or fish, or for adding very sparingly to a salad dressing. Genuine balsamic vinegar, known as *tradizionale,* is a glossy, rich, deep brown syrup. It is expensive but a little goes a long way.

VEGETABLES & SALADS

VEGETABLES GROW IN PROFUSION IN ITALY AND THE ITALIANS HAVE PUT THEIR HEART INTO USING THEM TO CREATE THE MOST IMAGINATIVE, TASTY, AND COLORFUL ANTIPASTI. BURSTING WITH FRESHNESS AND FLAVOR, VEGETABLES IN ANTIPASTI CAN BE SERVED RAW, DEEP-FRIED OR GRILLED, OR SLOWLY BAKED IN THE OVEN. WHETHER IT IS A SIMPLE DISH OF MARINATED BELL PEPPERS, A BOWL OF GLEAMING OLIVES, OR A SALAD WITH A ZESTY DRESSING, VEGETABLE ANTIPASTI WHET THE APPETITE WITHOUT OVERLOADING IT.

roasted bell peppers & tomatoes

peperoni arrostiti

2 red bell peppers

2 yellow bell peppers

2 orange bell peppers

4 tomatoes, halved

1 tbsp olive oil

3 garlic cloves, chopped

1 onion, sliced in rings

2 tbsp fresh thyme

salt and pepper

Packed with intense flavors, this vibrant, Mediterranean mix of bell peppers and tomatoes makes a colorful antipasto. It is also an excellent sauce for pasta or chicken. Serve with plenty of bread to mop up the garlicky juices.

Halve and seed the bell peppers. Place them, cut-side down, on a cookie sheet and cook under a preheated broiler for 10 minutes.

Add the tomatoes to the cookie sheet and broil for 5 minutes, until the skins of the bell peppers and tomatoes are charred.

Put the bell pepper into a polythene bag for 10 minutes to sweat, which will make the skin easier to peel.

Remove the tomato skins and chop the flesh. Peel the skins from the bell peppers and slice the flesh into strips.

Heat the oil in a large skillet and fry the garlic and onion, stirring occasionally, for 3–4 minutes or until softened.

Add the bell peppers and tomatoes to the skillet and cook for 5 minutes. Stir in the fresh thyme and season to taste with salt and pepper.

Transfer to serving bowls and serve warm or chilled.

eggplant rolls

involtini di melanzane

2 eggplant, sliced thinly
  lengthwise
5 tbsp olive oil
1 garlic clove, crushed
4 tbsp pesto
1½ cups mozzarella, grated
basil leaves, torn into pieces
salt and pepper
fresh basil leaves, to garnish

Sprinkle the eggplant slices liberally with salt and leave for 10–15 minutes to extract the bitter juices. Turn the slices over and repeat. Rinse well with cold water and drain on paper towels.

Heat the olive oil in a large skillet and add the garlic. Fry the eggplant slices lightly on both sides, a few at a time. Drain them on paper towels.

Spread the pesto onto one side of the eggplant slices. Top with the grated mozzarella and sprinkle with the torn basil leaves. Season with a little salt and pepper. Roll up the slices and secure with wooden toothpicks.

Arrange the eggplant rolls in a greased ovenproof baking dish. Place in a preheated oven, 180°C/350°F/Gas Mark 4, and bake for 8–10 minutes.

Transfer the eggplant rolls to a warmed serving plate. Scatter with fresh basil leaves and serve at once.

zucchini fritters

frittelle di zucchini

3¹/2 oz/100 g self–rising flour

2 eggs, beaten

2 fl oz/50 ml milk

10¹/2 oz/300 g zucchini

2 tbsp fresh thyme

1 tbsp oil

salt and pepper

Sift the self-rising flour into a large bowl and make a well in the center. Add the eggs to the well and, using a wooden spoon, gradually draw in the flour.

Slowly add the milk to the mixture, stirring continuously to form a thick batter.

Grate the zucchini over a few paper towels placed in a bowl to absorb some of the juices.

Add the zucchini, thyme, and salt and pepper to taste to the batter and mix thoroughly, for about a minute.

Heat the oil in a large, heavy-bottom skillet. Taking a tablespoon of the batter for a medium-size fritter or half a tablespoon of batter for a smaller-size fritter, spoon the mixture into the hot oil and cook, in batches, for 3–4 minutes on each side.

Remove the fritters with a slotted spoon and drain thoroughly on absorbent paper towels. Keep each batch of fritters warm in the oven while making the rest. Transfer to serving plates and serve hot.

mushrooms with roasted garlic & scallions

funghi con aglio e cipolline

2 garlic bulbs

2 tbsp olive oil

12 oz/350 g assorted mushrooms,
   such as cremini, open-cap, and
   chanterelles, halved if large

1 tbsp chopped fresh parsley

8 scallions, cut into 1-inch/
   2.5-cm lengths

salt and pepper

The mellow flavor of roasted garlic complements the earthiness of mushrooms. Roasting the garlic makes it irresistibly soft with a rich, mellow flavor, quite unlike raw or fried garlic.

Preheat the oven to 350°F/180°C/Gas Mark 4. Slice off the tops of the garlic bulbs and press down to loosen the cloves. Place them in an ovenproof dish and season to taste with salt and pepper. Drizzle 2 teaspoons of the oil over the bulbs and roast for 30 minutes. Remove from the oven and drizzle with 1 teaspoon of the remaining oil. Return to the oven and roast for an additional 45 minutes. Remove from the oven and let stand until cool enough to handle, then peel the cloves.

Tip the oil from the dish into a heavy-bottom skillet, add the remaining oil and heat. Add the mushrooms and cook over medium heat, stirring frequently, for 4 minutes.

Add the garlic cloves, parsley, and scallions and cook, stirring frequently, for 5 minutes. Season to taste with salt and pepper and serve at once.

tomato, mozzarella & avocado salad

insalata di pomodoro, mozzarella, e avocado

2 ripe beefsteak tomatoes

5¹/2 oz/150 g fresh mozzarella

2 avocados

4 tbsp olive oil

1¹/2 tbsp white wine vinegar

1 tsp coarse-grain mustard

few fresh basil leaves, torn into
 pieces

20 black olives

salt and pepper

fresh crusty bread, to serve

Using a sharp knife, cut the tomatoes into thick wedges and place in a large serving dish. Drain the mozzarella and coarsely tear into pieces. Cut the avocados in half and remove the pits. Cut the flesh into slices, then arrange the mozzarella and avocado with the tomatoes.

Mix the oil, vinegar, and mustard together in a small bowl, add salt and pepper to taste, then drizzle over the salad.

Sprinkle the basil and olives over the top and serve at once with fresh crusty bread.

green & white bean salad

insalata di fagioli bicolore

½ cup dried Great Northern
  beans, soaked overnight
8 oz/225 g fine green beans,
  trimmed
¼ red onion, thinly sliced
12 black olives, pitted
1 tbsp chopped chives

dressing

½ tbsp lemon juice
½ tsp Dijon mustard
6 tbsp extra virgin olive oil
salt and pepper

Drain the soaked beans and put in a saucepan with plenty of fresh water to cover. Bring to a boil, then boil rapidly for 15 minutes. Reduce the heat slightly and cook for a further 30 minutes, or until tender but not disintegrating. Add salt in the last 5 minutes of cooking. Drain and set aside.

Meanwhile, plunge the green beans into a large pan of boiling water. Bring back to a boil and cook for 4 minutes, until just tender but still brightly colored and crunchy. Drain and set aside.

Whisk together the dressing ingredients, then let stand.

While both types of bean are still slightly warm, tip them into a shallow serving dish or arrange on individual plates. Scatter over the onion slices, olives and chives.

Whisk the dressing again and spoon over the salad. Serve immediately, at room temperature, in a warmed bowl.

fava bean salad

insalata di fave

5 lb 8 oz/2.5 kg young fava beans
in their pods, shelled to give
about 14 oz/400 g, or
15 oz/425 g frozen baby
fava beans
2 tomatoes, peeled, seeded, and
diced
3 tbsp shredded basil
1¾ oz/50 g Parmesan shavings

dressing
1 tsp white wine vinegar
1 small garlic clove, crushed
4 tbsp extra virgin olive oil
salt and pepper

Diced tomatoes, Parmesan and a garlicky dressing contrast well with soft, starchy fava beans. A light scattering of basil adds freshness and color. The salad can be made ahead of time and positively benefits from standing at room temperature for a while.

Bring a large pan of water to a boil. Add the beans, bring back to a boil, then cook for 3 minutes, until just tender. Drain and tip into a serving dish or arrange on individual plates.

Whisk the dressing ingredients and spoon over the beans while still warm.

Scatter over the diced tomato, basil, and Parmesan shavings. Serve immediately, at room temperature, in a warmed bowl.

olives with orange & lemon

olive con l'arancio ed il limone

2 tsp fennel seeds

2 tsp cumin seeds

1¼ cups green olives

1¼ cups black olives

2 tsp grated orange rind

2 tsp grated lemon rind

3 shallots, finely chopped

pinch of ground cinnamon

4 tbsp white wine vinegar

5 tbsp extra virgin
  olive oil

2 tbsp orange juice

1 tbsp chopped fresh mint

1 tbsp chopped fresh parsley

Dry-roast the fennel seeds and cumin seeds in a small, heavy-bottom skillet, shaking the skillet frequently, until they begin to pop and give off their aroma. Remove the skillet from the heat and let cool.

Place the olives, orange and lemon rind, shallots, cinnamon, and roasted seeds in a bowl.

Whisk the vinegar, olive oil, orange juice, mint, and parsley together in a bowl and pour over the olives. Toss well, then cover and let chill for 1–2 days before serving.

MEATS

ITALY PRODUCES SOME OF THE WORLD'S FINEST CURED AND COOKED MEATS MADE ACCORDING TO TIME-HONORED TRADITIONS WITH SUPERB INGREDIENTS. OFFERING A RICH VARIETY OF FLAVORS AND TEXTURES, DOZENS OF SALAMI, AIR-DRIED AND BOILED HAMS, AND EXQUISITE REGIONAL SPECIALTIES FORM THE BASIS OF A TRADITIONAL ANTIPASTI PLATTER. PAPER-THIN SLICES OF BEEF FILLET, CURED LEG OF GOAT, SMOKED GOOSE, AND DUCK BREAST ARE SOME OF THE MORE UNUSUAL MEATS THAT ARE PARTICULARLY POPULAR IN THE NORTH.

mixed antipasto meat platter

antipasti misti di carne

1 cantaloupe

2 oz/55 g Italian salami, sliced
  thinly

8 slices prosciutto

8 slices bresaola

8 slices mortadella

4 plum tomatoes, sliced thinly

4 fresh figs, quartered

2/3 cup black olives, pitted

2 tbsp shredded fresh basil leaves

4 tbsp extra virgin olive oil, plus
  extra for serving

ciabatta loaf, sliced

pepper

Cut the melon in half, scoop out and discard the seeds, then cut the flesh into 8 wedges. Arrange the wedges on one half of a large serving platter.

Arrange the salami, prosciutto, bresaola, and mortadella in loose folds on the other half of the platter. Arrange the tomato slices and fig quarters along the center of the platter.

Sprinkle the olives and shredded basil over the platter and drizzle with olive oil. Season to taste with pepper, then serve with slices of ciabatta and extra olive oil, for dipping and drizzling.

marinated raw beef

carpaccio marinato

Paper-thin slices of raw beef fillet are transformed by a marinade of lemon juice and fruity olive oil. A sprinkling of parsley and sweet, nutty, Parmesan shavings add contrasting flavors. Since it is served raw, the beef must be the very best quality.

7 oz/200 g beef fillet, in one
  piece
2 tbsp lemon juice
4 tbsp extra virgin olive oil
1/2 cup Parmesan cheese, shaved
  thinly
4 tbsp chopped fresh flat-leaf
  parsley
salt and pepper
lemon slices, to garnish
fresh bread, to serve

Using a very sharp knife, cut the beef fillet into paper-thin slices and arrange on four individual serving plates.

Pour the lemon juice into a small bowl and season to taste with salt and pepper. Whisk in the olive oil, then pour the dressing over the meat. Cover the plates with plastic wrap and set aside for 10–15 minutes to marinate.

Remove and discard the plastic wrap. Arrange the Parmesan shavings in the center of each serving and sprinkle with parsley. Garnish with lemon slices and serve with fresh bread.

prosciutto with arugula

prosciutto e rucola

4 oz/115 g arugula

1 tbsp lemon juice

3 tbsp extra virgin olive oil

8 oz/225 g prosciutto, sliced
  thinly

salt and pepper

Separate the arugula leaves, wash in cold water, and pat dry on paper towels. Place the leaves in a bowl.

Pour the lemon juice into a small bowl and season to taste with salt and pepper. Whisk in the olive oil, then pour the dressing over the arugula leaves and toss lightly so they are evenly coated.

Carefully drape the prosciutto in folds on individual serving plates, then add the arugula. Serve at room temperature.

ham & salami with figs

prosciutto e salame con fichi

9–12 ripe figs, depending on size

6 thin slices dry-cured Italian ham

12 thin slices salami

1 small bunch of fresh basil,
  separated into small sprigs

few fresh mint sprigs

1 small bunch of arugula leaves

2 tbsp freshly squeezed lemon
  juice

4 tbsp extra virgin olive oil

salt and pepper

Trim the stems of the figs to leave just a short length, then cut the figs into quarters.

Arrange the ham and salami on a large serving platter.

Wash and dry the herbs and arugula and put in a bowl with the prepared figs.

Whisk the lemon juice and oil together with a fork in a small bowl and season well with salt and pepper. Pour over the herbs and salad greens and carefully turn the figs and greens in the dressing until they are well coated.

Spoon the figs and salad onto the meat and arrange around the platter.

mushrooms stuffed with bacon & spinach

funghi ripieni con spinaci e pancetta

Little nuggets of bacon with chopped spinach, garlic, and crisp, golden breadcrumbs make a superb stuffing for oven-baked mushrooms. They can be served straight from the oven, or prepared ahead of time and served at room temperature.

5 cups fresh baby spinach leaves

4 portobello mushrooms

3 tbsp olive oil

2 oz/55 g rindless bacon, finely
  diced

2 garlic cloves, crushed

1 cup fresh white or brown
  breadcrumbs

2 tbsp chopped fresh basil

salt and pepper

Preheat the oven to 400°F/200°C. Rinse the spinach and place in a pan with only the water clinging to the leaves. Cook for 2–3 minutes, until wilted. Drain, squeezing out as much liquid as possible, and chop finely. Cut the stalks from the mushrooms and chop finely, reserving the whole caps.

Heat 2 tablespoons of the oil in a skillet. Add the mushroom caps, rounded-side down, and cook for 1 minute. Remove from the skillet and arrange, rounded-side down, in a large ovenproof dish.

Add the chopped mushroom stalks, bacon, and garlic to the skillet and cook for 5 minutes. Stir in the spinach, breadcrumbs, basil, and salt and pepper to taste. Mix well and divide the stuffing among the mushroom caps.

Drizzle the remaining oil over the top and bake in the oven for 20 minutes, until crisp and golden.

chicken rolls with lemon & rosemary

involtini di pollo al limone e rosmarino

3 skinless, boneless chicken
  breasts, about 1 lb/450 g

finely grated zest of 1 lemon

1 tbsp chopped fresh rosemary

1/2 tsp coarse sea salt

1/4 tsp freshly ground black
  pepper

2¾ oz/75 g thinly sliced pancetta

4 tbsp vegetable oil

2 tbsp dry white wine

arugula or radicchio salad,
  to serve

Slice the chicken breasts in half horizontally to make six pieces. Place between two sheets of plastic wrap and pound with a mallet until thin. Try to make them roughly rectangular in shape, trimming the edges a little if necessary.

Spread the lemon zest and rosemary over one side of each piece of chicken. Season with the salt and black pepper. Roll up a chicken piece, wrap in one or two slices of pancetta and secure with a cocktail stick. Repeat for the rest of the chicken pieces.

Heat the oil in a pan large enough to take the rolls in a single layer. When the oil is hot but not smoking, add the rolls and cook over medium-high heat, turning often, until browned. Stir in the wine, reduce the heat to low, then cover and cook over medium-low heat for 15 minutes. Remove from the pan and drain on crumpled paper towels.

Remove the cocktail sticks and slice each roll in half. Serve warm or at room temperature with arugula or radicchio salad.

chicken morsels fried in batter

bocconcini di pollo pastellati

1 lb 2 oz/500 g skinless, boneless
  chicken thighs

3 tbsp olive oil

juice of 1/2 lemon

2 garlic cloves, crushed

8 tbsp all-purpose flour

vegetable oil for deep-frying

2 eggs, beaten

salt and pepper

coarsely chopped fresh flat-leaf
  parsley, to garnish

lemon wedges, to serve

Cut the chicken thighs into 1 1/2-inch/4-cm chunks. Mix the olive oil, lemon juice, garlic, and salt and pepper in a bowl. Add the chicken pieces and let marinate at room temperature for an hour, or overnight in the refrigerator.

Spread the flour on a plate and mix with a pinch of salt and plenty of pepper.

When ready to cook, remove the chicken pieces from the marinade and drain.

Heat the vegetable oil in a deep-fat fryer or large saucepan until a cube of bread browns in 20 seconds. Roll the chicken in the seasoned flour and then in beaten egg. Immediately drop into the hot oil, a few pieces at a time, and deep-fry for about 5 minutes, until golden and crisp, turning occasionally with tongs. Drain on crumpled paper towels.

Place the chicken pieces in a warmed serving dish and sprinkle with parsley. Serve hot with thick wedges of lemon.

braised chicken salad

insalata di pollo

3 tbsp olive oil

1 chicken, weighing about
  3 lb/1.3 kg

7 fl oz/200 ml dry white wine

1 onion, chopped

1 carrot, chopped

1 celery stalk, chopped

1 fresh bay leaf

salt and pepper

marinade

1 tsp black peppercorns

4 fresh bay leaves

4 fl oz/125 ml olive oil

salt

salad

5½ oz/150 g baby spinach leaves

5 tender celery stalks

1 head chicory

1 tsp wine vinegar

1 tsp balsamic vinegar

salt

This impressive summer antipasto can be prepared days in advance and is great for feeding a crowd. Tender shreds of marinated chicken are served on crisp baby spinach leaves, chicory, and diced celery. A drizzle of gleaming balsamic vinegar sharpens the flavors.

Preheat the oven to 350°F/180°C. Heat the olive oil in an ovenproof casserole over medium-high heat. Add the chicken and fry for 15 minutes, turning, until golden all over. Pour in the wine and simmer for 2 minutes, then add the onion, carrot, celery, and bay leaf. Season with salt and pepper. Cover tightly and transfer to the oven. Bake for 45–50 minutes, turning every 20 minutes, until the juices from the thickest part of the thigh run clear when pierced with a skewer. Discard the liquid and solids. When cool enough to handle, remove and discard the skin. Strip the meat from the bone, slicing any large chunks into bite-size pieces.

Arrange the chicken in a dish. Sprinkle with a little salt, a few peppercorns, and the bay leaves. Pour in enough oil to generously coat. Cover tightly with plastic wrap and marinate in the refrigerator for 1–2 days. Remove the chicken from the refrigerator 2 hours before serving. Place in a colander set over a bowl to drain, and leave to stand until the oil has liquefied.

To make the salad, chop the leaves as desired. Combine the spinach, celery, and chicory in a large serving dish. Toss with salt, enough oil from the chicken to just coat the leaves, and the wine vinegar. Arrange the chicken on top, discarding the peppercorns and bay leaves. Sprinkle with the balsamic vinegar before serving.

FISH & SEAFOOD

WITH OVER 4,000 KM OF COASTLINE, ITALY BOASTS AN ASTONISHING
VARIETY OF FISH AND SEAFOOD. IT'S HARDLY SURPRISING THAT THEY ARE KEY
INGREDIENTS IN SOME OF THE BEST ANTIPASTI, EVEN IN INLAND REGIONS. FROM THE
ROBUST RICHNESS OF TUNA AND SARDINES, TO THE CLEAN, SALTY TANG OF A SEAFOOD
SALAD (INSALATA DI MARE), THE CHOICE IS ENDLESS. SIMPLE TECHNIQUES SUCH AS
GRILLING, STEAMING, AND SEARING ENHANCE THE NATURAL, FRESH FLAVORS AND
INHERENT GOODNESS OF THE CATCH.

monkfish, rosemary & bacon skewers

spiedini di pescatrice, rosmarino, e pancetta

9 oz/250 g monkfish fillet

12 fresh rosemary stems

3 tbsp olive oil

juice of 1/2 small lemon

1 garlic clove, crushed

6 rindless thick Canadian bacon
   slices

salt and pepper

lemon wedges, to garnish

aïoli, to serve

Slice the fillet in half lengthwise, then cut each fillet into 12 bite-size chunks to give a total of 24 pieces. Put the monkfish pieces in a large bowl. To prepare the rosemary skewers, strip the leaves off the stems and set them aside, leaving a few leaves at one end.

For the marinade, finely chop the reserved leaves and whisk with the oil, lemon juice, garlic, and salt and pepper to taste in a nonmetallic bowl. Add the fish pieces and toss until coated in the marinade. Cover and let marinate in the refrigerator for 1–2 hours.

Cut each bacon slice in half lengthwise, then in half widthwise, and roll up each piece. Thread 2 fish pieces alternately with 2 bacon rolls onto the prepared rosemary skewers.

Preheat the broiler, griddle, or barbecue. If you are cooking the skewers under a broiler, arrange them on the broiler rack so that the leaves of the rosemary skewers protrude from the broiler and therefore do not catch fire during cooking. Cook the skewers, turning frequently and basting with any remaining marinade, for 10 minutes, or until cooked. Serve hot, garnished with lemon wedges for squeezing over, with some aïoli on the side.

seared tuna with white beans & artichokes

tonno con fagioli bianchi e carciofi

2/3 cup extra virgin olive oil

juice of 1 lemon

1/2 tsp dried chile flakes

4 thin fresh tuna steaks, weighing
about 1 lb/450 g

1¼ cups dried cannellini beans,
soaked overnight

1 shallot, finely chopped

1 garlic clove, crushed

2 tsp finely chopped rosemary

2 tbsp chopped flat-leaf parsley

4 oil-cured artichokes, quartered

4 vine-ripened tomatoes, sliced
lengthwise into segments

16 black olives, pitted

salt and pepper

lemon wedges, to garnish

Put 4 tablespoons of the olive oil in a shallow dish with 3 tablespoons of the lemon juice, the chile flakes, and ¼ teaspoon pepper. Add the tuna steaks and leave to marinate at room temperature for 1 hour, turning occasionally.

Meanwhile, drain the beans and put in a saucepan with plenty of fresh water to cover. Bring to a boil, then boil rapidly for 15 minutes. Reduce the heat slightly and cook for another 30 minutes, or until tender but not disintegrating. Add salt in the last 5 minutes of cooking.

Drain the beans and place in a bowl. While still warm, toss with 5 tablespoons of the olive oil, then stir in the shallot, garlic, rosemary, parsley, and remaining lemon juice. Season with salt and pepper to taste. Let stand for at least 30 minutes to allow the flavors to develop.

Heat the remaining oil in a skillet until very hot. Add the tuna and the marinade, and sear for 1–2 minutes each side over very high heat. Remove from the skillet and allow to cool a little.

Transfer the beans to a serving dish. Mix in the artichokes, tomatoes, and olives, adding more oil and seasoning if necessary. Flake the tuna and arrange on top. Garnish with lemon wedges and serve at room temperature.

marinated sardine fillets with oregano & fennel

filetti di sardina marinati con origano e finocchio

8 large fresh sardines, gutted and
   scaled

6 tbsp extra virgin olive oil

1 tbsp white wine vinegar

1 tbsp dried oregano

2 garlic cloves, crushed

1 tsp black peppercorns, crushed

1/2 tsp sea salt

1/4 tsp dried chile flakes

1/2 red onion, sliced thinly

1 fennel bulb, trimmed, quartered
   lengthwise, and thinly sliced

4 tomatoes, seeded and sliced into
   thin segments

2 tbsp shredded fresh basil

Italians love small tasty fish and this dish is typical of those served around the Bay of Naples, where the fish is particularly fresh and abundant. Fragrant oregano and crunchy slivers of fennel cut the richness of the sardines.

Preheat the oven to 350°F/180°C/Gas Mark 4. Place the sardines in an ovenproof baking dish. Combine the oil, vinegar, oregano, and garlic, and season with the peppercorns, sea salt, and chile flakes. Pour the mixture over the sardines. Bake for 20–25 minutes until the flesh is no longer translucent around the backbone.

Remove the sardines from the oven and leave to cool in the baking dish. Sprinkle with the red onion slices, cover with plastic wrap, and leave to marinate in the refrigerator for up to 3 days. Remove from the 1–2 hours refrigerator before serving.

Arrange the fennel and tomato segments on top of the sardines, spooning over some of the oily juices from the dish. Sprinkle with the basil just before serving.

anchovies with celery & arugula

alici con sedano e rucola

2 celery stalks, strings removed

4 small handfuls of arugula

12–16 brine-cured anchovy fillets,
   halved lengthwise

1½ tbsp extra virgin olive oil

salt and pepper

thick lemon wedges, to serve

Quarter the celery stalks lengthwise and slice into 3-inch/7.5-cm batons. Soak in ice-cold water for 30 minutes, until crisp and slightly curled, then drain and pat dry.

Place a small pile of arugula on individual serving plates. Arrange the celery and anchovy fillets attractively on top. Spoon over a little olive oil and season with salt and pepper, bearing in mind the saltiness of the anchovies. Serve with thick wedges of lemon.

baked scallops

capesante al forno

1 lb 9 oz/700 g shelled scallops,
   chopped
2 onions, finely chopped
2 garlic cloves, finely chopped
3 tbsp chopped fresh parsley
pinch of freshly grated nutmeg
pinch of ground cloves
2 tbsp fresh white breadcrumbs
2 tbsp olive oil
salt and pepper

Preheat the oven to 400°F/200°C. Mix the scallops, onions, garlic, 2 tablespoons of the parsley, the nutmeg, and cloves together in a bowl and season to taste with salt and pepper.

Divide the mixture between 4 scrubbed scallop shells or heatproof dishes. Sprinkle the breadcrumbs and remaining parsley on top and drizzle with the olive oil.

Bake the scallops in the preheated oven for 15–20 minutes, or until lightly golden and piping hot. Serve immediately.

pan-fried shrimp

gamberi in padella

4 garlic cloves

20–24 large, raw shrimp, peeled

8 tbsp butter

4 tbsp olive oil

6 tbsp brandy

salt and pepper

2 tbsp chopped fresh parsley,
  to garnish

lemon wedges, to serve

Beautiful pink shrimp are a feature of seafood antipasti platters all around Italy's extensive coastline. Here they are sizzled with finely sliced garlic in a rich sauce of olive oil, butter, and brandy. The shrimp must be top-quality and absolutely fresh.

Using a sharp knife, peel and slice the garlic.

Wash the shrimp and pat dry using paper towels.

Melt the butter with the oil in a large skillet, add the garlic and shrimp, and fry over high heat, stirring, for 3–4 minutes, until the shrimp are pink.

Sprinkle with brandy and season with salt and pepper to taste. Sprinkle with parsley and serve immediately with lemon wedges.

mixed seafood salad

insalata di mare

2 garlic cloves, crushed

juice of 1½ lemons

4 tbsp extra virgin olive oil

2 tbsp chopped fresh flat-leaf
  parsley

1 lb 5 oz/600 g cooked seafood
  cocktail (shrimp, mussels, clams,
  calamari rings, cockles)

1 oil-cured roasted red bell
  pepper, sliced into thin strips

12 black olives, pitted

2 tbsp shredded fresh basil

salt and pepper

Whisk the garlic, lemon juice, olive oil and parsley with salt and pepper to taste.

Drain the seafood if necessary, and tip into a serving dish. Add the bell pepper and olives, then mix with the garlic mixture, turning to coat. Leave in a cool place for 30 minutes to allow the flavors to develop.

Stir again before serving, check the seasoning, and sprinkle with the basil.

grilled shrimp with arugula & radicchio

gamberi ai ferri con rucola e radicchio

1 garlic clove, crushed

juice of 1/2 lemon

4 tbsp extra virgin olive oil

1/4 tsp dried chile flakes

9 oz/250 g large, raw, peeled
shrimp, without heads

8 radicchio leaves, sliced into
ribbons

4 handfuls arugula

1 tsp wine vinegar

2 tbsp shredded fresh basil

salt and pepper

Whisk the garlic and lemon juice with 3 tablespoons of the oil, the chile flakes, and salt and pepper to taste. Pour over the shrimp and leave to marinate for 30 minutes.

Put the radicchio and arugula in a bowl. Sprinkle with salt and pepper and toss with the remaining tablespoon of oil. Sprinkle with the vinegar and toss again. Divide the leaves among individual plates.

Preheat a grill pan over high heat. Add the shrimp and grill for 1–2 minutes, turning and brushing with the marinade, until uniformly pink. Arrange on top of the salad and sprinkle with the basil.

BREADS & PASTRIES

WHETHER SERVED WITH COLD MEATS OR SALADS, OR IN ITS OWN RIGHT AS BRUSCHETTA

OR CROSTINI, GOOD BREAD IS AN ESSENTIAL PART OF ANTIPASTI. THE MEAL CANNOT

BEGIN IN EARNEST UNTIL IT IS ON THE TABLE. OTHER DOUGH-BASED ANTIPASTI

INCLUDE CHICKPEA FLOUR CRÊPES (FARINATA) SOLD HOT IN WEDGES, SMALL PIZZAS

(PIZETTE), AND SAVORY TARTS (TORTINI) WITH MELTINGLY CRISP PASTRY AND TASTY

FILLINGS. EQUALLY TEMPTING ARE BITE-SIZE DEEP-FRIED PASTRIES (PANZEROTTI)

STUFFED WITH CHEESE AND HAM.

bruschetta with tomatoes

bruschetta al pomodoro

10 1/2 oz/300 g cherry tomatoes

4 sun-dried tomatoes

4 tbsp extra virgin olive oil

16 fresh basil leaves, shredded,
  plus extra leaves to garnish

2 garlic cloves, peeled

8 slices ciabatta

salt and pepper

Served all over Umbria, Tuscany, and central Italy, this deceptively simple antipasto relies on the very best ingredients: authentic ciabatta, sun-ripened cherry tomatoes, fresh garlic, and top-quality extra virgin olive oil.

Using a sharp knife cut the cherry tomatoes in half and the sun-dried tomatoes into strips. Place them in a bowl, add the olive oil and the shredded basil leaves, and toss to mix well. Season to taste with a little salt and pepper.

Using a sharp knife, cut the garlic cloves in half. Lightly toast the ciabatta bread.

Rub the garlic, cut-side down, over both sides of the lightly toasted ciabatta bread.

Top the ciabatta bread with the tomato mixture, garnish with basil leaves, and serve immediately.

mixed vegetable bruschetta

bruschetta alle verdure miste

olive oil, for brushing
   and drizzling

1 red bell pepper, halved
   and seeded

1 orange bell pepper, halved
   and seeded

4 thick slices ciabatta

1 fennel bulb, sliced

1 red onion, sliced

2 zucchini, sliced diagonally

2 garlic cloves, halved

1 tomato, halved

salt and pepper

fresh sage leaves, to garnish

Brush the grill pan with oil and place it over medium heat. Cut each bell pepper in half lengthwise into 4 strips. Toast the bread slices on both sides in a toaster or under a broiler.

When the grill pan is hot add the bell peppers and fennel and cook for 4 minutes, then add the onion and zucchini and cook for an additional 5 minutes, until all the vegetables are tender but still with a slight "bite". If necessary, cook the vegetables in 2 batches, as they should be placed on the grill pan in a single layer.

Meanwhile, rub the garlic halves over the toasts, then rub them with the tomato halves. Place on warmed plates. Pile the grilled vegetables on top of the toasts, drizzle with olive oil, and season with salt and pepper. Garnish with the sage and serve immediately.

wild mushroom bruschetta

bruschetta ai funghi selvatici

4 slices sourdough bread,
   such as Pugliese
3 garlic cloves, 1 halved and
   2 crushed
2 tbsp extra virgin olive oil
8 oz/225 g mixed wild
   mushrooms, such as porcini,
   chanterelles, and portobello
   mushrooms
1 tbsp olive oil
2 tbsp butter
1 small onion or 2 shallots,
   finely chopped
1/2 cup dry white wine
   or Marsala
salt and pepper
2 tbsp coarsely chopped fresh
   flat-leaf parsley, to garnish

Toast the bread slices on both sides, under a preheated broiler, or in a preheated ridged grill pan then rub with the garlic halves and drizzle with the extra virgin olive oil. Transfer to a cookie sheet and keep warm in a warm oven.

Wipe the mushrooms thoroughly to remove any trace of soil, and slice any large ones. Heat the olive oil with half the butter in a skillet, then add the mushrooms and cook over medium heat, stirring frequently, for 3–4 minutes, or until soft. Remove with a slotted spoon and keep warm in the oven.

Heat the remaining butter in the skillet and add the onion and crushed garlic, then cook over medium heat, stirring frequently, for 3–4 minutes, or until soft. Add the wine and stir well, then let bubble for 2–3 minutes, or until reduced and thickened. Return the mushrooms to the skillet and heat through. The sauce should be thick enough to glaze the mushrooms. Season to taste with salt and pepper.

Pile the mushrooms on top of the warm bruschetta, then sprinkle with the parsley and serve immediately.

cheese & sun-dried tomato toasts

toast al formaggio e pomodori secchi

2 sfilatini

¾ cup sun-dried tomato paste

10½ oz/300 g mozzarella,
   drained and diced

1¼ tsp dried oregano

2–3 tbsp olive oil

pepper

Italians use all kinds of artisan breads to give simple antipasti an extra-special quality. Here, the crisp, craggy texture of toasted sfilatino or ciabatta contrasts beautifully with the soft, creamy texture of mozzarella.

Preheat the oven to 425°F/220°C. Slice the loaves diagonally and discard the end pieces. Toast the slices on both sides under a preheated broiler until golden.

Spread one side of each toast with the sun-dried tomato paste and top with mozzarella. Sprinkle with oregano and season to taste with pepper.

Place the toasts on a large baking sheet and drizzle with olive oil. Bake in the preheated oven for about 5 minutes, until the cheese has melted and is bubbling. Remove the hot toasts from the oven and let stand for 5 minutes before serving.

crostini alla fiorentina

crostini alla fiorentina

3 tbsp olive oil

1 onion, chopped

1 celery stalk, chopped

1 carrot, chopped

1–2 garlic cloves, crushed

4½ oz/125 g chicken livers

4½ oz/125 g calf's, lamb's or

  pig's liver

⅔ cup red wine

1 tbsp tomato purée

2 tbsp chopped fresh parsley

3–4 canned anchovy fillets,

  chopped finely

2 tbsp stock or water

2–3 tbsp butter

1 tbsp capers

salt and pepper

small pieces of fried crusty bread,

  to serve

freshly chopped parsley, to

  garnish

Heat the oil in a pan, add the onion, celery, carrot and garlic, and cook gently for 4–5 minutes, or until the onion is soft but not colored.

Meanwhile, rinse and dry the chicken livers. Dry the calf's or other liver, and slice into strips. Add the liver to the pan and fry gently for a few minutes, until the strips are well sealed on all sides.

Add half of the wine and cook until it has mostly evaporated. Then add the rest of the wine, the tomato purée, half of the parsley, the anchovy fillets, stock or water, a little salt and plenty of black pepper.

Cover the pan and leave to simmer, stirring occasionally, for 15–20 minutes, or until tender and most of the liquid has been absorbed.

Leave the mixture to cool a little, then either coarsely mince or put into a food processor and process to a chunky purée.

Return to the pan and add the butter, capers and remaining parsley. Heat through gently until the butter melts. Adjust the seasoning and turn out into a bowl.
Serve warm or cold spread on the slices of crusty bread and sprinkled with freshly chopped parsley.

tomato & cheese tart

torta di pomodoro e formaggio

4½ oz/125 g white bread flour

4½ oz/125 g self-rising flour

4½ oz/125 g chilled butter

1 egg yolk

4 tbsp cold water

oil, for greasing

salt

filling

8–9 tomatoes, peeled, seeded, and
   cut into eighths

5½ oz/150 g coarsely grated
   Emmental cheese

4 eggs

3½ fl oz/100 ml heavy cream

2 tbsp chopped fresh oregano or
   marjoram

1 tbsp chopped fresh chives

salt and pepper

Sift the flours and salt into a bowl, then sift again to mix thoroughly. Dice the butter and work it into the flours, rubbing between your fingertips and thumbs until the mixture resembles dry sand. Beat together the egg yolk and water, and stir into the flour mixture with a fork. Once the dough starts to clump, knead very lightly to form a compact ball. Wrap in plastic wrap and place in the refrigerator for at least 30 minutes.

Preheat the oven to 325°F/160°C. Lightly grease an 11-inch/28-cm loose-bottom tart pan. Roll out the pastry very thinly and use to line the pan. Pass a rolling pin over the top of the pan to trim off surplus dough. Using the side of your forefinger, press the dough into the corner of the pan to raise it slightly above the rim. Line with greaseproof paper and weigh down with dried beans, making sure they go all the way to the edge. Bake blind for 15 minutes.

Arrange the tomato segments in the pastry shell in concentric circles. Sprinkle the grated cheese evenly over the top. Beat the eggs lightly, then stir in the cream, oregano, chives, and salt and pepper. Mix well, then pour into the pastry shell. Return to the oven and bake for 20–25 minutes, until puffy and golden. Serve hot or warm.

fried cheese pastries

sgonfiotti al formaggio

7 oz/200 g all-purpose flour, plus
    extra for dusting

2 eggs, lightly beaten

2 tbsp olive oil

1–2 tbsp cold water

1 egg white, beaten until slightly
    frothy

vegetable oil for deep-frying

salt

filling

4 1/2 oz/125 g ricotta cheese

1 egg, lightly beaten

2 1/2 oz/70 g mozzarella, diced
    finely

1 oz/25 g Parmesan cheese,
    diced finely

1 1/2 oz/40 g salami or Parma ham,
    chopped finely

1 tbsp chopped fresh flat-leaf
    parsley

salt and pepper

These tasty little pies were traditionally sold as street food in Rome. Served while still crisp and piping hot, they make an irresistible snack or antipasto. Fillings vary but usually include ham or salami and a good melting cheese such as mozzarella.

To make the filling, mix all the ingredients together in a bowl and season to taste. Sift the flour into a large bowl. Make a well in the center and pour in the eggs. Add the oil and a pinch of salt. Stir with a fork, gradually drawing in the flour from around the edge. Once a dough has formed, knead for about 10 minutes, until smooth and silky. Wrap the dough in plastic wrap and leave to rest in the fridge for at least 30 minutes or overnight.

Roll out the dough very thinly and, using a pastry cutter, stamp out circles about 2 3/4-inches/7-cm in diameter, re-rolling the dough until it is all used. Place the circles on a clean dish towel. Wet the edges of the circles with egg white. Place a teaspoon of filling in the middle, then fold over one half to form a semicircle. Press the edges together, making sure they stick. Let rest on the dish towel for 30 minutes.

Heat the vegetable oil in a deep-fat fryer or large saucepan and drop the pastries into the hot oil, a few at a time, deep-frying for about 3-5 minutes. Remove from the pan and drain on crumpled paper towels. Serve at once while still hot.

EGGS & CHEESE

A SELECTION OF ANTIPASTI WOULD NOT BE COMPLETE WITHOUT AN EGG DISH OR
SOMETHING MADE WITH CHEESE. HARD-COOKED EGG HALVES STUFFED WITH TANGY
FILLINGS ARE POPULAR, AS ARE WEDGES OF WARM OR COLD FRITTATA. IN THE NORTHERN
ALPS, SOFT CREAMY CHEESES ARE USED IN DIPS AND SPREADS. IN THE NORTH-EAST,
A SENSATIONALLY LARGE, CRISP FRITTER (FRICO) IS MADE WITH MONTASIO CHEESE.
CAMPANIA IN THE SOUTH IS FAMOUS FOR MILKY WHITE MOZZARELLA, SERVED
DEEP-FRIED BETWEEN SLICES OF BREAD.

spinach & ricotta patties

polpette di spinaci e ricotta

1 lb/450 g fresh spinach

9 oz/250 g ricotta cheese

1 egg, beaten

2 tsp fennel seeds, lightly crushed

1¾ oz/50 g pecorino or
Parmesan cheese, finely grated,
plus extra to garnish

1 oz/25 g all-purpose flour, mixed
with 1 tsp dried thyme

5 tbsp butter

2 garlic cloves, crushed

salt and pepper

tomato wedges, to serve

Wash the spinach and trim off any long stalks. Place in a pan, cover, and cook for 4–5 minutes, until wilted. This will probably have to be done in batches as the volume of spinach is quite large. Place in a colander and leave to drain and cool.

Mash the ricotta and beat in the egg and the fennel seeds. Season with plenty of salt and pepper, then stir in the pecorino cheese.

Squeeze as much excess water as possible from the spinach and finely chop the leaves. Stir the spinach into the cheese mixture.

Taking about 1 tablespoon of the spinach and cheese mixture, shape it into a ball and flatten it slightly to form a patty. Gently roll in the seasoned flour. Continue this process until all of the mixture has been used up.

Half-fill a large skillet with water and bring to a boil. Carefully add the patties and cook for 3–4 minutes, or until they rise to the surface. Remove with a slotted spoon.

Melt the butter in a pan. Add the garlic and cook for 2–3 minutes. Pour the garlic butter over the patties, season with pepper, and serve at once with the tomato wedges, and garnished with the grated cheese.

mushroom & taleggio tarts

tartellette ai funghi e taleggio

1 lb/450 g prepared puff pastry

all-purpose flour, for dusting

5 tbsp olive oil, plus extra for
   brushing

1 lb 9 oz/700 g red onions, thinly
   sliced

9 oz/250 g cremini mushrooms,
   sliced

2 tbsp pine nuts

1 tbsp chopped fresh oregano

3½ oz/100 g Taleggio cheese,
   sliced

salt and pepper

Roll out the pastry on a floured counter and cut out four 5-inch/12½-cm squares. Let chill for 30 minutes. Place 2 baking sheets in the oven and preheat to 425°F/220°C.

Meanwhile, heat 3 tablespoons of the oil in a skillet. Add the onions and cook gently for 30 minutes, until caramelized. Remove from the skillet and let cool.

Heat the remaining oil in the skillet. Add the mushrooms and cook over high heat until softened and the liquid has evaporated. Let cool, then stir into the onions. Mix in the pine nuts, oregano, and salt and pepper.

Place the chilled pastry squares on the baking sheets. Prick the pastry squares with a fork and brush with oil. Divide the mushroom mixture among them, leaving a ½-inch/1-cm margin. Arrange the cheese on the top. Bake for 15 minutes, until the pastry is golden and risen and the cheese has melted.

figs with bleu cheese

fichi e gorgonzola

3½ oz/100 g superfine sugar

4 oz/115 g whole almonds,
   blanched or unblanched

12 ripe figs

12 oz/350 g bleu cheese,
   crumbled

extra virgin olive oil

Plump juicy figs, caramelized almonds, and piquant bleu cheese are a mouthwatering combination. Try robust and spicy Gorgonzola bleu cheese or the milder dolcelatte, both from Lombardy in northern Italy.

First make the caramelized almonds. Put the sugar in a saucepan over medium–high heat and stir until the sugar melts and turns golden brown and bubbles; do not stir once the mixture starts to bubble. Remove from the heat and add the almonds one at a time and quickly turn with a fork until coated; if the caramel hardens, return the saucepan to the heat. Transfer each almond to a lightly buttered cookie sheet once it is coated. Leave until cool and firm.

To serve, slice the figs into quarters and arrange 8 quarters on each plate. Coarsely chop the almonds by hand. Place a mound of bleu cheese on each plate and sprinkle with chopped almonds. Drizzle the figs very lightly with the oil.

deep-fried mozzarella

mozzarella in carrozza

8 slices bread, preferably slightly
  stale, crusts removed
4 oz/100 g mozzarella, sliced
  thickly
⅓ cup chopped black olives
8 canned anchovy fillets, drained
  and chopped
16 fresh basil leaves
4 eggs, beaten
⅔ cup milk
oil, for deep-frying
salt and pepper

Cut each slice of bread into 2 triangles. Top 8 of the bread triangles with equal amounts of the mozzarella slices, olives, and chopped anchovies.

Place the basil leaves on top and season with salt and pepper to taste.

Lay the other 8 triangles of bread over the top and press down round the edges to seal.

Mix the eggs and milk together and pour into an ovenproof dish. Add the sandwiches and leave to soak for about 5 minutes.

Heat the oil in a large saucepan to 350–375°F/180–190°C, or until a cube of bread browns in 30 seconds.

Before cooking the sandwiches, squeeze the edges together again.

Carefully place the sandwiches in the oil and deep-fry for 2 minutes, or until golden, turning once. Remove the sandwiches with a slotted spoon and drain on paper towels. You will have to cook the sandwiches in batches. Serve immediately while still hot.

spinach & mozzarella omelet

omelette agli spinaci e mozzarella

1 tbsp butter

4 eggs, beaten lightly

1½ oz/40 g mozzarella, thinly
  sliced and cut into bite-size
  pieces

small handful baby spinach, stalks
  removed

salt and pepper

1 oil-cured red bell pepper, sliced
  into strips, to garnish

Heat a 10-inch/25-cm non-stick skillet over medium–high heat. Add the butter and when it sizzles, pour in the eggs. Season with salt and pepper, then stir gently with the back of a fork until large flakes form. Leave to cook for a few seconds then tilt the skillet and lift the edges of the mixture with a spatula, so that uncooked egg flows underneath.

Scatter the cheese and spinach over the top, and leave to cook for a few seconds. Once the surface starts to solidify, carefully fold the omelet in half. Cook for a few seconds, pressing the surface with a spatula. Turn the omelet over and cook for another few seconds, until the cheese is soft and the spinach wilted.

Slip the omelet onto a warm serving dish and slice into segments. Garnish with strips of bell pepper before serving.

piquant stuffed eggs

uova ripiene piccante

6 eggs

3 tbsp pesto sauce

¼ tsp Dijon mustard

2 tsp finely chopped fresh flat-leaf
  parsley

2 tsp capers, rinsed, drained, and
  chopped roughly

salt and pepper

dried chile flakes, and sprigs of
  fresh cilantro to garnish

Hard-cooked egg halves stuffed with piquant seasonings are a traditional antipasto found all over Italy. Here, tangy capers, pesto sauce, and cooked egg yolks make an attractive stuffing produced in very little time from pantry ingredients.

Put the eggs in a saucepan and cover with cold water. Bring to a boil and boil for 5 minutes. Drain and leave to cool. Shell the eggs and slice in half lengthwise. Carefully remove the yolks and set aside the whites.

Put the yolks in a bowl and mash with a fork. Stir in the pesto sauce, mustard, parsley, and capers. Season with pepper and a very little salt, bearing in mind the saltiness of the capers. Spoon the mixture into the egg white halves and sprinkle with chile flakes and cilantro sprigs.

artichokes with chive mayonnaise

carciofi con maionese aromatica

4 globe artichokes

1 lemon, halved

2 eggs, plus 2 yolks

¼ tsp dry mustard

8 fl oz/225 ml sunflower oil

4 tbsp chopped fresh chives, plus
   extra to garnish

salt and pepper

Using a very sharp knife, slice the stalks and tips from the artichokes. Rub the cut surfaces with a lemon half to prevent discoloration. Trim the tips of the remaining leaves with scissors. Place the artichokes in a bowl of water to which you have added the juice of the half lemon. Set aside the remaining piece of lemon. Bring a saucepan of water to a boil. Add the artichokes, weighing them down with a heatproof plate to keep them submerged. Bring back to a boil, then boil for 30-40 minutes. Drain and place upside down on a plate to cool.

Meanwhile, put the two whole eggs in a small saucepan and cover with cold water. Bring to a boil and boil for 5 minutes. Drain and leave to cool. Shell the boiled eggs and slice in half lengthwise. Separate the yolks from the whites and put them in a mixing bowl with the two raw yolks. Beat the yolks for 1 minute until smooth and sticky. Beat in the mustard, a pinch of salt, and a teaspoon of juice from the reserved lemon half. Add the oil, drop by drop, beating with each addition. Once the mixture starts to thicken, add the oil in a continuous thin stream, beating continuously. Thin with a little more lemon juice when all the oil is used up. Stir in the chopped chives and season with salt and pepper. Add more lemon juice if necessary.

Using a pointed teaspoon, scoop out the hairy "choke" from the middle of the artichokes. To serve, place the artichokes on individual plates and sprinkle with chopped chives. Serve the mayonnaise in a separate dish.